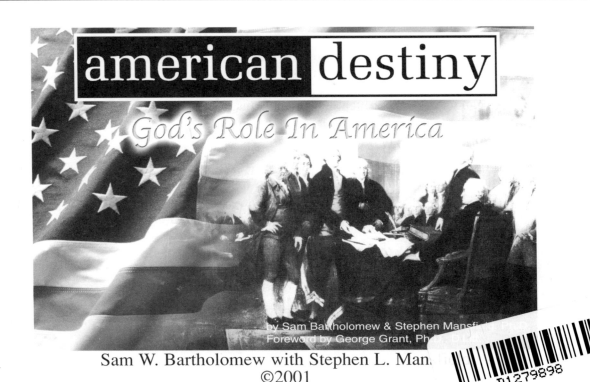

american destiny

God's Role In America

by Sam Bartholomew & Stephen Mansfield, Ph.D.
Foreword by George Grant, Ph.D., D.Litt.

Sam W. Bartholomew with Stephen L. Mansfield
©2001

ISBN - 0-9704986-0-8 (previously published by Eggman - 1-886371-31-8)

Published by: American Destiny Press
9 Music Square South
Suite 202
Nashville, TN. 37203
(615)895-1919
E-Mail - info@americandestiny.com

Cover Design by: Dieter Spears - inhauscreative@earthlink.net
(INHOUSE)

Printed in the United States of America ISBN - 0-9704986-0-8

"It is the duty of all nations to acknowledge the providence of Almighty God."

—George Washington

"We have grown in numbers, wealth, and power as no other nation has ever grown. But we have forgotten God."

—Abraham Lincoln

How to Use This Book

Because the quotations in the book generally appear in chronological order, it should be a useful tool for teaching U.S. history in the broad sense. Obviously, we are writing about the spiritual nature of famous Americans.

It also should be useful for speakers who would like to use Godly quotes from notable and historic Americans.

The book is intended to be easy reading, and we hope it will be used in the classrooms of our schools to provoke thought and discussion on the role of religion in America's history. Most important, we hope it will stir interest and debate on the subject of morality.

Politically, the book provides bipartisan examples of Godly leaders and hopefully it will encourage new candidates and provide ammunition for proper reading of the legislative intent of our Constitution and other founding documents.

ACKNOWLEDGMENTS

I would like to thank my family, particularly my Bible teacher wife, Vicki, for her persevering faith and heart for the Lord. Also, my long-suffering legal secretary and assistant, Peggy Cardwell, who puts up with much.

Also, a special thanks to Ambassador Joe M. Rodgers, whose Christian enthusiasm and deep concern for America helped make this work happen. He has been an inspiration to both Stephen and me.

—Sam Bartholomew

For enduring my many dreams and projects, most recently this one, I wish to thank my wife, Patricia. She, and my children, Jonathan and Elizabeth, are my treasures and my heart. My assistant, Jackie Lusk, has again brought her incredible gifts into harness on this project and I am thankful for all she is as well as all she gives. To my mentors—Dr. Rousas Rushdoony, Dr. George Grant, and Dr. Don Finto—I owe an eternal debt. *Deo Soli Gloria.*

—Stephen Mansfield

FOREWORD

The great English journalist, poet, and social critic Hilaire Belloc once asserted, "To comprehend the history of a thing is to unlock the mysteries of its present,
and more, to disclose the profundities of its future." But we moderns are enamored
of progress. We live at a time when things shiny and new are prized far above things
old and time-worn. For most of us, an appreciation of history is little more than a
quirky and nostalgic sentimentalism. It is hardly more than the droning, monotonous
succession of obsolete notions, anachronous ideals, and antiquarian habits—sound
and fury, signifying nothing. Henry Ford called an awareness of history and an
appreciation for the past mere "bunk." Augustine Birrell called it "a dust heap." Guy
de Maupassant dubbed it "that excitable and lying old lady." But the wisest of men
and women through the ages have always recognized that a discernment of the foundations of the past is the only sure footing upon which true advancement may be
built—that it is in fact, the prerequisite to all genuine progress. As Winston Churchill
asserted, "The greatest advances in human civilization have come when we recovered what we had lost: when we learned the lessons of history."

In this small collection of quotations, maxims, and epigrams, Sam Bartholomew and Stephen Mansfield have afforded us all a proper initial foothold for progress. They have reminded us of just what America once stood for. They have recovered for us the essential American character. They have revealed the principles that enabled this nation's great experiment in liberty to flower and flourish. And as a result, they have shown the way to our great American destiny.

It was Woodrow Wilson who said that, "A nation which does not remember what it was yesterday, does not know what it is today, nor what it is trying to do. We are trying to do a futile thing if we do not know where we came from or what we have been about. Ours is a rich legacy. Rich but lost." Now, thanks to Sam Bartholomew the statesman and Dr. Stephen Mansfield the historian, the process of recovering that rich legacy is just that much surer.

–George Grant

American Destiny, Inc. For a more in depth study of America's Christian roots, log on to www.AmericanDestiny.com

About Us - American Destiny Inc. is an educational organization which is non-profit, non-partisan, and non-denominational.

Our Mission - The mission of American Destiny is to challenge all Americans to remember God's hand in the founding and sustaining of our nation, by raising national awareness via billboards and mass media advertising, and to equip individuals to restore the heart and soul of America, via our website, conferences, and publications. It is our mission to pass history's torch of truth to the next generation of Americans.

Our Website - American Destiny.com is an Internet educational tool serving as gateway to a library of links and resources regarding America's founding. The following is a small sample of what you will find when you log on to American Destiny.com

- Read what our Founding Fathers actually said
- View America's founding documents
- Visit the homes of our Founding Fathers
- Discover God's role in America
- Learn what you can do to serve your country
- Recommended reading & Bookstore
- Links and Resources A-Z

American Destiny.com
9 Music Square S., Suite 202
Nashville, Tn 37203 (615) 895-1919
E-mail - info@americandestiny.com

www.americandestiny.com

11

QUOTATIONS

"And I say that Your Highnesses ought not to consent that any foreigner does business or sets foot here, except Christian Catholics, since this was the end and the beginning of the enterprise, that it should be for the enhancement and glory of the Christian religion, nor should anyone who is not a good Christian come to these parts."

Christopher Columbus wrote these words about America on November 27, 1492. He was the Christian mariner who inspired Europe with a vision for the New World. Many consider this the purpose of Western civilization.

"It was the Lord who put into my mind (I could feel his hand upon me) the fact that it would be possible to sail from here to the Indies. All who heard of my project rejected it with laughter, ridiculing me. There is no question that the inspiration was from the Holy Spirit, because He comforted me with the rays of marvelous inspiration from the Holy Scriptures . . ."

"I am a most unworthy sinner, but I have cried out to the Lord for grace and mercy, and they have covered me completely. I have found the sweetest consolation since I made it my whole purpose to enjoy His marvelous presence. For the execution of the journey to the Indies, I did not make use of intelligence, mathematics or maps. It is simply the fulfillment of what Isaiah had prophesied . . ."

These words were written by Christopher Columbus in his *Book of Prophecies*, a compilation of studies on the Scriptures completed after his third voyage to the New World.

"We, greatly commending, and graciously accepting of, their Desires for the Furtherance of so noble a Work, which may, by the Providence of Almighty God, hereafter tend to the Glory of his Divine Majesty, in propagating of Christian Religion to such People, as yet live in Darkness and miserable Ignorance of the true Knowledge and Worship of God, and may in time bring the Infidels and Savages, living in those Parts, to human Civility, and to a settled and quiet Government; Do, by these our Letters Patents, graciously accept of, and agree to, their humble and well-intended Desires."

This document, the First Charter of Virginia, written in 1606, clearly presents the vision that moved men to settle the New World.

". . . a great hope and inward zeal . . . of laying some good foundation, or at least to make some way thereunto, for the propagating and advancing of the Gospel of the kingdom of Christ in those remote parts of the world; yea, though they should be but even as stepping stones unto others for the performing of so great a work."

These words were written by William Bradford, Pilgrim father and governor of Plymouth, in his history of the colony, *Of Plimoth Plantation*.

"In The Name of God, Amen. . . .
Having undertaken for the Glory of God, and
Advancement of the Christian Faith, and the
Honour of our King and Country, a Voyage to
plant the first colony in the northern parts of
Virginia, Do by these Presents, solemnly and
mutually in the Presence of God and one another,
covenant and combine ourselves together into a
civil Body Politick . . ."

This statement was written by the Pilgrims on the Mayflower on November 11, 1620, just hours before they landed in the New World. Part of what is known as the Mayflower Compact, it clearly states the reason these early settlers risked so much to build a nation in the New World.

GOD'S ROLE IN AMERICA

"... Let every Student be plainly instructed, and earnestly pressed to consider well, the main end of his life and studies is, to know God and Jesus Christ which is eternal life, John 17:3, and therefore to lay Christ in the bottom, as the only foundation of all sound knowledge and learning. And seeing the Lord only giveth wisdom, Let every one seriously set himself by prayer in secret to seek it of him. Proverbs 2:3."

As with all of the leading colonial schools, these standards for Harvard University, first printed in the *Rules and Precepts of Harvard* in 1642, show how distinctly Christian the students were expected to be. Most of our great academic institutions were similarly Christian-based.

"Whereas we all came into these parts of America with one and the same end and aim, namely, to advance the Kingdom of our Lord Jesus Christ and to enjoy the liberties of the Gospel in purity and peace; and whereas in our settling (by wise providence of God) we are further dispersed upon the sea coasts and rivers than was at first intended."

Stating clearly the reason they voyaged to the New World, the Puritans who wrote this New England Confederation covenanted together for the purposes of God in the New World on May 19, 1643.

"The colonies are to pursue with peace
and loyal minds their sober, serious,
and religious intentions . . .
in holy Christian faith. . . .
A most flourishing civil state may stand
and best be maintained . . .
with a full liberty in religious concernments . . .
rightly grounded upon Gospel principles."

This passage is from the 1663 Royal Charter of Rhode Island, written by Roger Williams. The charter established broad religious tolerance in that colony.

"All scholars shall live religious, godly, and blameless lives according to the Rules of God's Word, diligently reading the holy Scriptures the Fountain of Light and truth; and constantly attend upon all the Duties of Religion both in public and secret."

These requirements, described in the *Laws of 1745* at Yale University, display the high intellectual and spiritual achievements required of scholars in the colonial period of this country.

*"Upon these two foundations,
the law of nature and
the law of revelation (the Bible),
depend all human laws."*

These words were written by William Blackstone, eminent British Jurist and legal scholar, in his *Commentaries on the Laws of England* in 1765. His writings were extremely influential in shaping the legal philosophy of the American colonies and our current system of jurisprudence.

*"The Christian Protestant religion
shall be deemed, and is hereby constituted
and declared to be,
the established religion of the State. . . .
No person should be eligible to a seat in the Senate
unless he be of the Protestant religion. . . ."*

As with almost all of the early state constitutions, South Carolina's Constitution reflects a solidly Christian world view.

*"Everyone appointed to public office must say,
I do profess faith in God the Father,
and in the Lord Jesus Christ his only Son,
and in the Holy Ghost, one God
and blessed forevermore;
and I do acknowledge the Holy Scriptures
of the Old and New Testaments
to be given by divine inspiration."*

Most of the colonies were distinctly Christian in matters of law and government, and when they became states, their Constitutions reflected this Biblical foundation. This quote is from the Delaware Constitution, framed in 1776.

*"Religion, or the duty which we owe
to our Creator and the manner of discharging it,
can be directed only by reason and conviction,
not by force or violence; and therefore all men
are equally entitled to the free exercise of religion,
according to the dictates of conscience. . . .
It is the mutual duty of all
to practice Christian forbearance,
love, and charity towards each other."*

These words are from Patrick Henry, firebrand of the American Revolution and governor of the Commonwealth of Virginia. He is well-known for his quote, "Give me liberty or give me death."

"It cannot be emphasized
too strongly or too often
that this great nation was founded,
not by religionists,
but by Christians,
not by religions,
but by the gospel of Jesus Christ."

This statement was made by Patrick Henry, who was powerfully influenced by the preaching of George Whitefield, the great British evangelist.

*"I have now disposed of all my property
to my family; there is one thing more
I wish I could give them,
and that is the Christian religion.
If they had this, and I had not given them
one shilling, they would be rich;
but if they had not that,
and I have given them all the world,
they would be poor."*

In a manner typical of the Founding Fathers, Patrick Henry wrote these words in his will, which his children heard upon his death in 1799.

GOD'S ROLE IN AMERICA

*"Principally, and first of all,
I resign my soul to the Almighty Being
who gave it,
and my body I commit to the dust,
relying on the merits of Jesus Christ
for the pardon of my sins."*

This confession was made by Samuel Adams. The fiery Adams led the Boston Tea Party and served in the Continental Congress.

*"We have this day restored the Sovereign
to Whom alone men ought to be obedient.
He reigns in heaven and . . .
from the rising to the setting sun,
may His kingdom come."*

This moving statement was made by Samuel Adams just moments after the thirteen colonies voted to separate from England on July 2, 1776.

GOD'S ROLE IN AMERICA

"The only foundation for . . .
a republic is to be laid in Religion.
Without this there can be no virtue,
and without virtue there can be no liberty,
and liberty is the object and life
of all republican governments."

These are the words of Benjamin Rush, colonial physician and college professor, who also signed the Declaration of Independence in 1776.

Excerpts from The Declaration of Independence

". . . When in the Course of human events, it becomes necessary for one people to dissolve the political bands which have connected them with another, and to assume among the Powers of the earth, the separate and equal station to which the Laws of Nature and of Nature's God entitle them, a decent respect to the opinions of mankind requires that they should declare the causes which impel them to the separation.

. . . We hold these truths to be self-evident, that all men are created equal, that they are endowed by their Creator with certain unalienable Rights, that among these are Life, Liberty, and the pursuit of Happiness.

. . . do, in the Name, and by Authority of the good People of these Colonies, solemnly publish and declare, that these United Colonies are, and of Right ought to be Free and Independent States; that they are Absolved from all Allegiance to the British Crown, and that all political connection between them and the State of Great Britain, is and ought to be totally dissolved; and that as Free and Independent States, they have full Power to levy War; conclude Peace, contract Alliances, establish Commerce, and to do all other Acts and Things which Independent States may of right do. And for the support of this Declaration . . ."

From The Declaration of Independence, The Unanimous Declaration of the Thirteen United States of America. In Congress, July 4, 1776.

GOD'S ROLE IN AMERICA

*"We hold sacred the rights of conscience,
and . . . promise the whole people . . . the free and
undisturbed exercise of their religion, but the right
to hold office is to be extended to persons of any
Christian denomination."*

This strong statement was made by Roger Sherman, the only Founder to sign all four of the founding documents.

"You do well to wish to learn our arts and our ways of life, and above all, the religion of Jesus Christ . . . Congress will do everything it can to assist you in this wise intention."

These words were spoken by George Washington to the Chiefs of the Delaware Indian tribe.

"It would be peculiarly improper to omit, in this official act, my fervent supplication to that Almighty Being, who rules over the universe, who presides in the council of nations, and whose providential aid can supply every human defect, that His benediction may consecrate to the liberties and happiness of the people of the United States. . . . Every step by which they have advanced seems to have been distinguished by some providential agency. We ought to be no less persuaded that the propitious smiles of Heaven can never be expected on a nation that disregards the eternal rules of order and right which Heaven itself has ordained."

George Washington, our first president, routinely prayed and offered thanks to God in his public speeches and statements, as this quote indicates.

"O most glorious God, in Jesus Christ . . . I acknowledge and confess my faults, in the weak and imperfect performance of the duties of this day. I have called on Thee for pardon and forgiveness of sins, but so coldly and carelessly that my prayers are come my sin and stand in need of pardon. I have heard Thy holy word, but with such deadness of spirit that I have been an unprofitable and forgetful hearer. . . . Let me live according to those holy rules which Thou hast this day prescribed in Thy holy word. . . . Direct me to the true object, Jesus Christ the way, the truth and the life. Bless, O Lord, all the people of this land."

This is an example of the prayers of George Washington, a strong Christian leader who served as a vestryman in his Episcopalian church.

"Almighty God; We make our earnest prayer that Thou wilt keep the United States in Thy holy protection; that Thou wilt incline the hearts of the citizens to cultivate a spirit of subordination and obedience to government; and entertain a brotherly affection and love for one another and for their fellow citizens of the United States at large.

And finally that Thou wilt most graciously be pleased to dispose us all to do justice, to love mercy, and to demean ourselves with that charity, humility, and pacific temper of mind which were the characteristics of the Divine Author of our blessed religion, and without a humble imitation of whose example in these things we can never hope to be a happy nation. Grant our supplication, we beseech Thee, through Jesus Christ our Lord. Amen."

Like many of the other Founding Fathers, George Washington is often accused of being a Deist. This prayer from his own handwritten prayer book shows the real nature of Washington's faith.

"And let us with caution indulge the supposition that morality can be maintained without religion. Whatever may be conceded to the influence of refined education on minds of peculiar structure, reason and experience both forbid us to expect that national morality can prevail in exclusion of religious principle."

In his famous Farewell Address, George Washington clearly stated one of his most heartfelt beliefs: that religious principles and personal character are inseparable. During the 1800s and much of the 1900s this Farewell Address was required reading in most public schools.

"He who shall introduce
into public affairs principles
of primitive Christianity
will change the face of the world."

Benjamin Franklin spoke these wise words while he was the American ambassador to France during the American Revolution.

"As to Jesus of Nazareth . . .
I think his system of Morals
and his Religion,
as he left them to us,
the best the world ever saw
or is likely to see."

As an ardent student of ethics and morals, Benjamin Franklin, inventor and respected leader of America's Continental Congress, drew this conclusion after studying the life and teachings of Jesus Christ.

"I've lived, sir, a long time, and the longer I live,
the more convincing proofs I see of this truth:
That God governs in the affairs of men.
If a sparrow cannot fall to the ground without His notice,
is it probable that an empire can rise without His aid?
We've been assured in the sacred writings
that unless the Lord build the house,
they labor in vain who build it.
I firmly believe this, and I also believe that
without His concurring aid,
we shall succeed in this political building
no better than the builders of Babel."

Even though he was in his eighties, Benjamin Franklin had a tremendous influence on the Constitutional Convention delegates.

"Statesmen . . . may plan and
speculate for liberty,
but it is Religion and Morality alone,
which can establish the Principles
upon which Freedom can securely stand . . ."

As a leading statesman of his day, John Adams's views about the relationship between religion and freedom are of great importance. He was the first vice-president under the Constitution and the second president of the United States.

> *"Our Constitution was made only for a moral and religious people. It is wholly inadequate to the government of any other."*

This astounding statement was made by John Adams, who understood as well as any man of his generation the vision of the Founding Fathers.

*"Is it not that the Declaration of Independence
first organized the social compact
on the Foundation
of the Redeemer's mission upon earth?
That it laid the cornerstone of human government
upon the first precepts of Christianity?"*

John Adams was a signer of the Declaration of Independence and its leading
advocate in debate. These words show the reason the document evoked such passion
in him.

"The only sure and permanent foundation of virtue is religion. Let this important truth be engraven upon your heart."

Though they sound like the ideas of a seasoned statesman, these words are from the pen of Abigail Adams, wife of President John Adams.

*"Can the liberties of a nation be thought secure
when we have removed their only firm basis,
a conviction in the minds of the
people that their liberties are the gift of God?"*

These words of Thomas Jefferson, our third president, are inscribed inside the Jefferson Memorial in Washington D.C. Jefferson also published a book, *The Ethics of Jesus of Nazareth*, which he gave to virtually all those working in government at the time.

"No people ought to feel greater obligations to celebrate the goodness of the Great Disposer of events and of the destiny of nations than the people of the United States. His kind providence originally conducted them to one of the best portions of the dwelling place allotted for the great family of the human race. He protected and cherished them under all the difficulties and trials to which they were exposed in their early days. Under His fostering care their habits, their sentiments, and their pursuits prepared them for a transition in due time to a state of independence and self-government . . ."

These words are not from the sermon of a pastor, but rather from the pen of James Madison, father of the Bill of Rights and fourth president of the United States.

"...Before any man can be considered as a member of Civil Society, he must be considered as a subject of the Governor of the universe."

James Madison, who once planned to study for the ministry, reflected the views of his generation in these words. Madison is called the "Architect of the Constitution."

"Let us humbly commit our righteous
cause to the great Lord of the Universe . . .
Let us joyfully leave our concerns in
the hands of Him who raises up
and puts down the empires and kingdoms
of the earth as He pleases."

This passionate plea is by John Hancock, president of the Continental Congress that officially drafted the Constitution and signer of the Declaration of Independence.

*"No man can be a sound lawyer
in this land
who is not well read in
the ethics of Moses
and the virtues of Jesus."*

The author of these words was leading colonial American jurist Fisher Ames. Ames, also a well-known orator and publicist, was so advanced that he graduated from Harvard at the age of sixteen.

"Providence has given to our people
the choice of their rulers,
and it is the duty . . . of a Christian nation
to select and prefer Christians
for their rulers."

This strong opinion was that of John Jay, diplomat, governor of New York, and for five years the first chief justice of the United States Supreme Court.

"No human society has ever been able to maintain both order and freedom, both cohesiveness and liberty apart from the moral precepts of the Christian Religion applied and accepted by all the classes. Should our Republic ever forget this fundamental precept of governance, men are certain to shed their responsibilities for licentiousness and this great experiment will then surely be doomed."

John Jay's words exemplify the Founding Father's belief that religion and public morality are inseparable.

"Religion, morality, and knowledge,
being necessary to good government
and the happiness of mankind,
schools and the means of education
shall forever be encouraged."

Several months before the completion and signing of the Constitution, its authors wrote this statement in the Northwest Ordinance, signed on July 13, 1787. Had the founders included a similar statement on religion and education in our Constitution, its later interpretations in these areas could have been dramatically different.

"Where there is no religion, there is no morality. . . . With the loss of religion . . . the ultimate foundation of confidence is blown up; and of life, liberty and property are buried in ruins."

These words are from a sermon given by Timothy Dwight, the president of Yale, on July 4, 1798.

"Religion and liberty are the meat and the drink of the body politic. Withdraw one of them and it languishes, consumes, and dies. . . .
Without religion we may possibly retain the freedom of savages, bears, and wolves, but not the freedom of New England.
If our religion were gone, our state of society would perish with it, and nothing would be left."

Timothy Dwight, the author of these words, was the grandson of colonial pastor Jonathan Edwards. He served as president of Yale in the early 1800s and led the school in revival during his years there.

"The patriot who feels himself in the service of God, who acknowledges Him in all his ways, has the promise of Almighty direction, and will find His Word in his greatest darkness, a 'lantern to his feet and a lamp unto his paths.' He will therefore seek to establish for his country in the eyes of the world, such a character as shall make her not unworthy of the name of a Christian nation."

These words were spoken on February 22, 1812, by American lawyer Francis Scott Key, composer of the *Star Spangled Banner.*

GOD'S ROLE IN AMERICA

*"The Christian religion is the religion
of our country.
From it are derived our prevalent notions
of the character of God,
the great moral governor of the universe.
On its doctrines are founded
the peculiarities of our free institutions."*

Spoken by William McGuffey, compiler of *McGuffey's Reader*, a series of schoolbooks that stressed religion and Godly character for generations of Americans during the 1800s.

"The moral principles and precepts contained in the scriptures ought to form the basis of all our civil constitutions and laws. All the miseries and evils which men suffer from vice, crime, ambition, injustice, oppression, slavery, and war, proceed from their despising or neglecting the precepts contained in the Bible."

These words were penned by Noah Webster, famed American educator and founding father who compiled the *American Dictionary of the English Language* in 1828.

God's Role in America

> ## *"Whatever makes a man a good Christian also makes a good citizen."*

In these words, Daniel Webster, early American educator and Secretary of State, expressed the view of his generation.

"If we and our posterity shall be true
to the Christian religion, if we and they shall live always
in the fear of God and shall respect His Commandments
. . . we may have the highest hopes
of the future fortunes of our country . . .
but if we and our posterity neglect religious instruction
and authority, violate the rules of eternal justice, trifle
with the injunctions of morality, and recklessly destroy
the political constitution which holds us together, no
man can tell how sudden a catastrophe may overwhelm
us that shall bury all our glory in profound obscurity."

Daniel Webster was known for his fiery oratory, particularly when his subject was the place of Christianity in America.

GOD'S ROLE IN AMERICA

"Probably at the time of the adoption of the Constitution, and of the amendment to it now under consideration, the general, if not the universal sentiment was, that Christianity ought to receive encouragement from the state, so far as was not incompatible with the private rights of conscience and the freedom of religious worship. An attempt to level all religions, and to make it a matter of state policy to hold all in utter indifference, would have created universal disapprobation, if not universal indignation."

This opinion of Judge Joseph Story would appear to be of great legal importance in determining legislative intent. Judge Story was not only a leading Constitutional scholar but also served on the Supreme Court from 1811 to 1845.

". . . there is no country in the world where the Christian religion retains a greater influence over the souls of men than in America; and there can be no greater proof of its utility and of its conformity to human nature than that its influence is powerfully felt over the most enlightened and free nation of the earth."

Alexis de Tocqueville was a noted French historian who wrote extensively on America in the early 1800s. He was greatly impressed by the Christian faith of the American people.

"I sought for the greatness and genius of America in her commodious harbors and her ample rivers, and it was not there; in her fertile fields and boundless prairies, and it was not there; in her rich mines and her vast world commerce, and it was not there. Not until I went to the churches of America and heard her pulpits aflame with righteousness did I understand the secret of her genius and power. America is great because she is good and if America ever ceases to be good, America will cease to be great."

In *Democracy in America*, Alexis de Tocqueville wrote of the powerful imprint of Christianity upon America's national life. These words are a moving testament to his search for the meaning of the nation.

"I do not know whether all Americans have a sincere faith in their religion—for who can know the human heart? —but I am certain that they hold it to be indispensable for the maintenance of republican institutions. The opinion is not peculiar to a class of citizens or to a party, but it belongs to the whole rank of society. America is the place where the Christian religion has kept the greatest power over men's souls; and nothing better demonstrates how useful and natural it is to man, since the country where it now has the widest sway is both the most enlightened and the freest."

As these words reveal, Alexis de Tocqueville was touched by the role of religion in the lives of Americans largely because his own country, France, had rejected the public influence of Christianity in its Revolution.

"The time has come that Christians must vote for honest men, and take consistent ground in politics or the Lord will curse them. . . . God cannot sustain this free and blessed country, which we love and pray for, unless the church will take right ground."

During the early 1800s, in potent terms such as these, Charles Finney preached about the social obligations that follow Christian conversion. His ministry moved thousands to take responsibility for the needs of their society.

"The highest glory of the American Revolution was this; it connected in one indissoluble bond, the principles of the civil government with the principles of Christianity. From the day of the Declaration . . . they [the American people] were bound by the laws of God, which they all, and by the laws of The Gospel, which they nearly all, acknowledged as the rules of their conduct."

John Quincy Adams, son of the second president and himself the sixth president of the United States, witnessed the events of the American Revolution and understood its meaning, as these words reveal.

"The first and almost the only Book deserving of universal attention is the Bible."

These words of John Quincy Adam, America's sixth president, are typical of the beliefs of many American presidents.

*"Whenever the pillars of Christianity
shall be overthrown,
our present republican forms of government,
and all the blessings which flow from them,
must fall with them."*

The sentiments of Jedediah Morse, called the "Father of American Geography." He was also the father of Samuel Morse, inventor of the telegraph and "Morse Code."

"Sir, I am in the hands of a merciful God.
I have full confidence in his goodness and mercy.
. . . The Bible is true. I have tried to conform to its
spirit as near as possible. Upon that sacred volume
I rest my hope for eternal salvation,
through the merits and blood of
our blessed Lord and Saviour, Jesus Christ."

President Andrew Jackson does not have a reputation as a particularly Godly man, but these words reveal the vibrant faith that lived in his heart and shaped his life.

"I nightly offer up my prayers to the throne
of grace for the health and safety of you all,
and that we ought all to rely with confidence
on the promises of our dear Redeemer,
and give Him our hearts, this is all he requires and
all that we can do, and if we sincerely do this,
we are sure of salvation through his atonement."

This statement was made by Andrew Jackson in a letter to his son at the end of his life.

GOD'S ROLE IN AMERICA

"It is impossible to mentally or socially enslave a Bible-reading people."

This statement by Horace Greeley represents the high regard for Scripture found in the American people. Greeley was a journalist, statesman, and the founder of the *New York Tribune*.

"The government of the United States is acknowledged by the wise and good of other nations, to be the most free, impartial, and righteous government of the world; but all agree that for such a government to be sustained many years, the principles of truth and righteousness, taught in the Holy Scriptures,must be practiced. The rulers must govern in the fear of God, and the people obey the laws."

These words by Emma Willard, educator, author and poet, were written in her *History of the United States* of 1843.

GOD'S ROLE IN AMERICA

"I fervently invoke the aid of
that Almighty Ruler
of the Universe
in whose hands
are the destinies of nations."

Reflecting the faith in God's sovereignty that has powered so much of American history, President James K. Polk spoke these words in his inaugural address on March 4, 1845.

"We are a Christian people . . . not because the law demands it, not to gain exclusive benefits or to avoid legal disabilities, but from choice and education; and in a land thus universally Christian, what is to be expected, what desired, but that we shall pay due regard to Christianity?"

This passage is from a report by the Senate Judiciary Committee, Congress of the United States, on January 19, 1853.

"Knowing that intercessory prayer is our mightiest weapon and the supreme call for all Christians today, I pleadingly urge our people everywhere to pray. Believing that prayer is the greatest contribution that our people can make in this critical hour, I humbly urge that we take time to pray—to really pray. Let there be prayer at sunup, at noonday, at sundown, at midnight—all through the day. Let us all pray for our children, our youth, our aged, our pastors, our homes. Let us pray for our churches.Let us pray for ourselves, that we may not lose the word 'concern' out of our Christian vocabulary. Let us pray for our nation. Let us pray for those who have never known Jesus Christ and redeeming love, for moral forces everywhere, for our national leaders. Let prayer be our passion. Let prayer be our practice."

General Robert E. Lee, commander of the Army of the Confederate States during the U.S. Civil War, was a man of prayer who often called upon his soldiers to cry out to God.

*"Unless the great God who assisted [Washington]
shall be with me and aid me, I must fail;
but if the same Omniscient Mind and Mighty Arm
that directed and protected him
shall guide and support me,
I shall not fail. . . .
Let us all pray that the God of our fathers
may not forsake us now."*

Abraham Lincoln, America's sixteenth president, spoke these words when he assumed the leadership of a divided nation.

GOD'S ROLE IN AMERICA

"But for [the Bible]
we could not know right from wrong.
All things most desirable for men's welfare . . .
are to be found portrayed in it."

Abraham Lincoln's faith in the Bible is typical of his times. Lincoln loved to read Scripture and often found comfort in its pages, as these words reveal.

"We have been the recipients of the choicest bounties of heaven. We have been preserved, these many years, in peace and prosperity. We have grown in numbers, wealth and power, as no other nation has ever grown. But we have forgotten God. We have forgotten the gracious hand which preserved us in peace, and multiplied and enriched and strengthened us; and we have vainly imagined, in the deceitfulness of our hearts, that all these blessings were produced by some superior wisdom and virtue of our own. Intoxicated with unbroken success, we have become too self-sufficient to feel the necessity of redeeming and reserving grace, too proud to pray to the God thus! It behooves us, then to humble ourselves before the offended Power, to confess our national sins and to pray for clemency and forgiveness."

These words are from Abraham Lincoln's Thanksgiving proclamation of April 30, 1860.

"The Almighty has His own purposes. Woe unto the world because of offenses; for it must needs be that offenses come, but woe to that man by whom the offense cometh.' If we shall suppose that American slavery is one of those offenses which, in the providence of God, must needs come, but which, having continued through His appointed time, He now wills to remove, and that He gives to both North and South this terrible war as the woe due to those by whom the offense came, shall we discern therein any departure from those divine attributes which the believers in a living God always ascribe to Him? Fondly do we hope, fervently do we pray, that this mighty scourge of war may speedily pass away. Yet, if God wills that it continue until all the wealth piled by the bondsman's two hundred and fifty years of unrequited toil shall be sunk, and until every drop of blood drawn with the lash shall be paid by another drawn with the sword, as was said three thousand years ago, so still it must be said, The judgments of the Lord are true and righteous altogether."

This paragraph is from Abraham Lincoln's Second Inaugural Address, which reveals his distinctly spiritual view of the Civil War.

"All the distinctive features and superiority of our republican institutions are derived from the teachings of Scripture."

Edward Everett was an American ambassador, the governor of Massachusetts, a Secretary of State, and U.S. senator. He spoke these words in a speech he delivered moments before Abraham Lincoln gave the famous Gettysburg Address.

"I know not how long a republican government can flourish among a great people who have not the Bible. . . . But this I do know: that the existing government of this country never could have had existence but for the Bible. And, further, I do in my conscience believe that if at every decade of years a copy of the Bible could be found in every family in the land, its republican institutions would be perpetuated."

These words were penned by William Seward, U.S. senator, governor of New York, and secretary of state under Abraham Lincoln.

*"The American government and Constitution
is the most precious possession which the world
holds, or which the future can inherit.
This is true—true because the American system
is the political expression of Christian ideas."*

This statement from the North American Review of 1867 summarizes well the beliefs of both the Founders of America and the generations that followed them.

"Let us look forward to the time
when we can take the flag of our country
and nail it below the Cross, and there let it wave
as it waved in the olden times,
and let us gather around it
and inscribe for our motto:
'Liberty and Union, one and inseparable,
now and forever,' and exclaim:
Christ first, our country next."

These words are a powerful testament to the confidence of Andrew Johnson,
America's seventeenth president, and his age that America was a Christian nation.

*"Hold fast to the Bible as
the sheet-anchor of your liberties;
write its precepts in your
hearts and practice them in your lives.
To the influence of this book
we are indebted for all the progress
made in true civilization and to this
we must look as our guide in the future."*

This exhortation is from Ulysses S. Grant, eighteenth president of the United States and commander of the Northern Armies during the American Civil War.

*"Men who see not God in our history have surely
lost sight of the fact that,
from the landing of the Mayflower to this hour,
the great men whose names are indissolubly
associated with the colonization, rise,
and progress of the Republic
have borne testimony to the
vital truths of Christianity."*

Henry Wilson served in the U.S. Senate from 1855 to 1873 and was vice-president during the presidency of Ulysses S. Grant. His words represent the thinking of generations of American Christians.

"I am a firm believer in the Divine teachings, perfect example, and atoning sacrifice of Jesus Christ. I believe also in the Holy Scriptures as the revealed Word of God to the world for its enlightenment and salvation."

This creed is from Rutherford B. Hayes, the nineteenth president of the United States.

"Our laws and our institutions must necessarily be based upon and embody the teachings of the Redeemer of mankind. It is impossible that it should be otherwise; and in this sense and to this extent our civilization and our institutions are emphatically Christian. . . . This is a religious people. This is historically true. From the discovery of this continent to the present hour, there is a single voice making this affirmation . . . we find everywhere a clear recognition of the same truth. . . . These, and many other matters which might be noticed, add a volume of unofficial declarations to the mass of organic utterances that this is a Christian nation."

This affirmation by U.S. Supreme Court Justice David Brewer, in the case of *Church of the Holy Trinity* vs. *United States*, on February 29, 1892, reflects what was for generations an accepted fact of American life.

*"In this actual world,
a churchless community,
a community where men have abandoned
and scoffed at, or ignored their Christian duties,
is a community on the rapid down-grade."*

President Theodore Roosevelt, America's twenty-sixth president, was an eminent historian who understood the decline of a people who lose their religious and moral foundation. This quote shows his belief in the "Christian duties" as essential to a successful community.

*"The Bible . . . is the one supreme source of
revelation of the meaning of life,
the nature of God and spiritual nature
and need of men. It is the only guide of life
which really leads the spirit
in the way of peace and salvation."*

Woodrow Wilson, the son of a Presbyterian minister, served as president of
Princeton, governor of New Jersey, and twenty-eighth president of the United States.

"I firmly believe in Divine Providence.
Without belief in Providence I think
I should go crazy.
Without God the world
would be a maze without a clue."

President Woodrow Wilson shaped much of the modern world armed with this belief in the sovereignty of God. He was president during "the war to end all wars"—World War I.

"It is my conviction that the fundamental trouble with the people of the United States is that they have gotten too far away from Almighty God."

This quotation illustrates the belief of Warren G. Harding, the twenty-ninth president of the United States.

"The foundations of our society and our government rest so much on the teachings of the Bible that it would be difficult to support them if faith in these teachings would cease to be practically universal in our country."

With these words, Calvin Coolidge, the thirtieth president of the United States, expressed the faith of many in his generation.

"The whole inspiration of our civilization springs from the teachings of Christ and the lessons of the prophets. To read the Bible for these fundamentals is a necessity of American life."

These words were written in 1943 by then former President Herbert Hoover in a joint statement with Mrs. Calvin Coolidge, Mrs. Theodore Roosevelt, Mrs. William H. Taft, Mrs. Benjamin Harrison, and Mrs. Grover Cleveland.

"We cannot read the history of our rise and development as a nation, without reckoning with the place the Bible has occupied in shaping the advances of the Republic. . . . Where we have been the truest and most consistent in obeying its precepts, we have attained the greatest measure of contentment and prosperity."

These words were spoken by President Franklin Roosevelt in a 1935 radio broadcast to the nation. Roosevelt was president during World War II.

"The basis of our Bill of Rights comes from the teachings we get from Exodus and St. Matthew, from Isaiah and St. Paul. I don't think we emphasize that enough these days. If we don't have a proper fundamental moral background, we will finally end up with a . . . government which does not believe in rights for anybody except the State!"

In understanding American government this way, Harry Truman, the thirty-third president, reflected the philosophies of the Founding Fathers.

"A person who is fundamentally honest
doesn't need a code of ethics.
The Ten Commandments and
the Sermon on the Mount
are all the ethical code anybody needs."

These are the words of Harry S. Truman, often known as "Give 'em Hell Harry."

"Our government makes no sense unless it is founded on a deeply felt religious faith."

General Dwight Eisenhower, who became the thirty-fourth president, spoke these words during the Korean Conflict when many Americans were uncertain about what distinguished their nation. He had our Pledge of Allegiance modified to include the words "one nation under God."

*"We are a religious people
and our institutions presuppose
a Supreme Being."*

With these words, noted liberal Supreme Court Justice William O. Douglas simply restated the intentions of the Founding Fathers that America be "one nation under God."

*"Whoever tries to conceive the American
word without taking full account of the suffering
and love and salvation of Christ is only dreaming.
I know how embarrassing this matter is to
politicians, bureaucrats, businessmen and cynics;
but, whatever these honored men think,
the irrefutable truth is that the soul of America
is at its best and highest, Christian."*

These words were spoken by Charles Malik, ambassador to the United Nations from Lebanon and president of the U.N. General Assembly.

"Without God there could be no American form of government, nor an American way of life. Recognition of the Supreme Being is the first— the most basic—expression of Americanism. Thus the founding fathers of America saw it, and thus with God's help, it will continue to be."

These words were spoken by Gerald R. Ford, the thirty-eighth president of the United States, on December 5, 1974.

GOD'S ROLE IN AMERICA

"I was ... a Sunday school teacher and a deacon, and I professed to be quite concerned about my religious duties. But when asked that question [whether there was enough evidence to convict me of being a Christian] I finally decided that if arrested ... I could probably talk my way out of it! It was a sobering thought."

President Jimmy Carter, our thirty-ninth president, was an outspoken Baptist. He brought modern controversy concerning the term *born again* to the White House.

"[Our Founders] . . . came in search of religious freedom. Landing on a desolate shoreline, they established a spiritual foundation that has served us ever since. It was the hard work of our people, the freedom they enjoyed and their faith in God that built this country and made it the envy of the world. In all of our great cities and towns, evidence of the faith of our people is found: houses of worship of every denomination are among the oldest structures."

President Ronald Reagan reveals in these words not only his own understanding of the greatness of America but one shared by generations of Americans.

GOD'S ROLE IN AMERICA

"The frustrating thing is that those who are attacking religion claim they are doing it in the name of tolerance, freedom, and open-mindedness. Question: Isn't the real truth that they are intolerant of religion? They refuse to tolerate its importance in our lives."

This quote is from a speech by Ronald Reagan, the fortieth president of the United States.

"...*I know that this is in our reach because we are guided by a power larger than ourselves who creates us equal in His image... We are not this story's author who fills time and eternity with His purpose. Yet his purpose is achieved in our duty, and our duty is fulfilled in service to one another.*"

President George W. Bush in his Inaugural address January 20th 2001

GOD'S ROLE IN AMERICA

Appendix A

Statute passed by Tennessee legislature in 1993 and signed by the governor.

49-6-1011. Historical documents, writings and records — Use in classrooms — Censorship prohibited.— (a) No teacher or administrator in a local education agency shall be prohibited from using or reading from, during the course of educational instruction, or from posting in a public school building, classroom or event, any of the following or any excerpts or portions of the following:

(1) The national motto;
(2) The national anthem;
(3) The Pledge of Allegiance;
(4) The Constitution of Tennessee;
(5) The Declaration of Independence;

(6) The writings, speeches, documents, and proclamations of the founders, presidents of the United States, or the founders or governors of Tennessee;

(7) Opinions of the United States and Tennessee supreme courts; and

(8) Acts of the United States congress and acts of the Tennessee general assembly.

(b) The list of historically significant or venerated documents, writings or records set out in subsection (a) shall not be construed to be exclusive, and the doctrine of ejusdem generis shall not be applied to prohibit the use, reading or posting of other such documents, writings or records.

(c) The use, reading or posting of the types of documents, writings and records authorized by this section shall be undertaken for educational purposes only and shall not be used to promote or establish any religion or religious belief.

(d) There shall be no content-based censorship of American or Tennessee history or heritage based on any religious references contained in such documents, writings or records. [Acts 1993. ch. 116, § 1.]

(Kentucky has passed a similar statute)

GOD'S ROLE IN AMERICA

Appendix B
Sources and Recommended Reading

The quotations used in this booklet are largely in the public domain in the letters, speeches, and official papers of American leaders. Others are from Associated Press news stories and the books listed below. Because most readers will never venture into the unfamiliar territory of original sources, the following list has been developed to point out some of the most informative and interesting books on the subject of American Christian history.

The Light and the Glory by Peter Marshall and David Manuel (Old Tappan: Fleming H. Revell Company, 1977)

This book is the absolute best introduction to a Christian view of the founding of America and the first centuries of settlement. Readers will be introduced to the spiritual lives of such people as Christopher Columbus and George Washington. A children's version is also available.

From Sea to Shining Sea by Peter Marshall and David Manuel (Old Tappen:
 Fleming H. Revell Company, 1986)

This is the second volume of the series begun by *The Light and the Glory*. The
authors cover the period from the American Revolution to the Civil War with the
same skill and passion they poured into the first volume. A children's version is also
available.

Faith and Freedom: The Christian Roots of American Liberty by Benjamin Hart
(San Bernardino: Here's Life Publishers, 1988)

An interesting, well-written overview of the major spiritual and theological
forces in the founding and settling of America.

America: To Pray or Not to Pray? by David Barton (Aledo, TX: WallBuilder Press,
1988)

David Barton's materials are essential for understanding the role of Christian
faith and prayer in the American experience.

The Christian History of the Constitution of the United States of America by Verna Hall (San Francisco: Foundation for American Christian Education, 1966)

An excellent compilation of original writings and biographies that help to explain the background of the U.S. Constitution.

The Christian Legal Advisor by John Eidsmoe (Milford: Mott Media, 1984)

Although this book is a practical guide for navigating the American legal system, it contains hundreds of pages dealing with the character, faith, and philosophy of the Founding Fathers.

Political Sermons of the American Founding Era, 1730-1805, Ellis Sandoz, ed. (Indianapolis: Liberty Press, 1991)

An immensely helpful volume of sermons from the religious leaders who laid the spiritual foundation of the nation.

Real Threat and Mere Shadow: Religious Liberty and the First Amendment by Daniel L. Dreisbach (Westchester: Crossway Books, 1987)

This is an excellent analysis of the philosophical background, original intent, and modern perversion of the First Amendment.

Dictionary of Christianity in America, Daniel G. Reid, ed. (Downers Grove: InterVarsity Press, 1990)

With more than 2,400 informative articles, this dictionary is a much needed reference for an important field that few people really understand.

America's God and Country: Encyclopedia of Quotations by William J. Federer (Fame Publishing, Inc., Coppell, 1994)

A comprehensive compendium of short biographies and quotes highlighting the Christian influences of great Americans from all walks of life.

INDEX

A
Adams, Abigail 45
Adams, John 42, 43, 44
Adams, Samuel 29, 30
Adams, John Quincy 66, 67
Ames, Fisher 50

B
Blackstone, William 23
Bradford, William 17
Brewer, David 87

C
Carter, Jimmy 101
Columbus, Christopher 14, 15
Coolidge, Calvin 92

D
De Tocqueville, Alexisa 62, 63, 64
Declaration of Independence 32
Delaware Constitution 25
Douglas, William O. 98
Dwight, Timothy 54, 55

E
Eisenhower, Dwight 97

Everett, Edward 80

F
Finney, Charles 65
First Charter Of Virginia 16
Ford, Gerald 100
Franklin, Benjamin 39, 40, 41

G
Grant, Ulysses S. 84
Greeley, Horace 71

H
Hancock, John 49
Harvard University 19
Harding, Warren G. 91
Hayes, Rutherford B. 86
Henry, Patrick 26, 27, 28
Hoover, Herbert 93

J
Jackson, Andrew 69, 70
Jay, John 51, 52
Jefferson, Thomas 46
Johnson, Andrew 83